Published in Great Britain by Stafford Pemberton Publishing Limited,
Ruskin Chambers, Drury Lane, Knutsford, Cheshire
Printed in Italy
ISBN 0 86030 352 7

Contents **Page**

Photographs Supplied by John Dawes and Published Courtesy of Limited, Manchester.
Designed and Produced by Back to the Drawing Board

WORLD OF SPORT ANNUAL 1983

Ray Clemence.

Hello and welcome to this World of Sport Annual. I hope you find it as interesting and varied as the programme that we produce. Every Saturday of almost every year.

As a matter of fact, if you've got this book as a Christmas present, you might like to ponder on the fact that it'll be the first time in six years that I'll be relaxing on a Saturday afternoon – except for holidays, that is!

What our production team tries to achieve in the programme is a mixture of sport that is taken seriously, and at top levels, but not always the obvious ones.

So it was World of Sport that pioneered the coverage of darts — with the News of the World Final, from the cauldron of beer and enthusiasm that was Wembley ten years ago. They said it couldn't be covered — WOS not only proved that it was magical, instant TV, but helped experts like Eric Bristow and John Lowe into the superstar (not to mention super-tax) bracket. We also sought events from round the world that were rarely seen over here.

The general principle that we believed in was that if thousands, hundreds of thousands, and even millions, of people in other countries could be besottedly keen on any sports event, there must be something in them which could be transmitted to British audiences.

A case in point is the Tour de France, which is arguably the world's greatest annual sports gathering. Phil Liggett talks about it elsewhere in the Annual, but the whole TV presentation is a most remarkable technical achievement, and now astonishingly smooth. The cameramen, with the light-weight electronic equipment who race along at thirty-odd miles an hour beside the cyclists are obviously great experts. Spare a thought for the motor bike drivers, who not only have to anticipate the breaks that the cyclists are going to make and understand the complicated tactics of the race, but, generally, to avoid interfering with it. Spectators are horrifyingly close to the action, and the riders are naturally concentrating on their own problems. Yet the close-ups the cameramen get are some of the most remarkable in sport of men under stress — obeying the old cycling rule that the winner is the one who is able to suffer most.

Another event that we regularly show is the Australian Rules football final from Melbourne. There are upwards of a hundred thousand spectators for this annual high-scoring Aussie ritual. First-time viewers are often baffled by the strange-looking goal, with two pairs of posts, the punched passes and the dribbling with the ball bounced off the instep. In the end, the fact that one doesn't understand all the finer points somehow doesn't matter, as one is carried into the exhilaration of the action. Much the same applies to the American Football Superbowl, maybe the most glamorous event of the North American sporting year. As with much American sport, the home commentary is technical and statistical — we believe that our English commentary team makes the game generally understandable, without losing any of that typically American razzmatazz.

I was out in Canada for the Calgary Stampede — and went big game fishing as well, for World of Sport. That was superb, but, as I've suggested, Saturdays are mostly about being in the Kent House studio, which London Weekend TV owns. The team is based here at the South Bank; it's right next door to the National Theatre and the National Film Theatre. Somehow, the idea of a "cultural village" in the area hasn't yet come into being, but we have an impressive array of buildings — and of output — it's a bit like being in the middle of an artistic industrial estate.

Just to explain; ITV is a collection of independent companies, who take some programmes from the ITV network. World of Sport is a network show, based at LWT but it has the ability to take items *from* the rest of the network, rather than just feed out. So we bring for instance racing from Yorkshire, motor cycling from Donington (which is Central) and sailing from TVS. There are soccer reports from all the regional companies available to us, depending on the game's importance, and often sound reports from other matches provided by the Independent radio companies.

The complexity of the operation is flabbergasting, and I rely on the production team here to give me exactly the right sort of information. When you see me on air, I'm wearing a "deaf aid" — that's to say, a radio-linked talk-back receiver — in my ear, into which the Production Assistants are counting the seconds into the next piece of film or video, Director Patricia Mordecai is telling me what is available, and the Editor (probably Andrew Franklin) is telling me the latest news.

Also coming up with information are other members of the production team, with scores and results for future reference. The messengers pick up details from the Agency machines which you can see in the background; the sub-editors are constantly on the 'phone to freelance journalists on the grounds at important matches. Their stories are correlated, and given to the typists (yes, they really *work,* and, very hard too) who provide me with a constant stream of information.

Getting all this together can occasionally (but luckily rarely) result in the odd moment of confusion. I once was given the impression that a story had been ditched, and threw it away under my desk — I must have the widest waste-bin in the world! Then it was re-instated, and suddenly I heard the dread words: "Coming to Dickie . . . five . . . four . . . three . . . two . . . one". Not normally too much to worry about, but at that moment, I was still under my desk, scrabbling for that elusive story!

One of the elements which has helped to make our programme much quicker off-the-mark than we were is what we call "Capgen" and "Bettmak" — the two electronic typewriters that now put up superimpositions of names at the bottom of the frame, provide latest soccer scores, and, most importantly, give us racing results so much more quickly than when they all had to be hand-written.

So World of Sport is always trying to produce a slicker and more informative programme, without making it seem too mechanical and plastic — always a danger when new electronic toys are to hand. The Olympic motto is "faster, higher, stronger". Theories that this is how the team like their after-the-show snifters are quite wrong. We like to think our key-words are "neater, newsier, and more fun".

Good viewing in '83, with World of Sport.

WORLD

The beaches of Europe were a little quieter this summer, but if you went into an Italian restaurant you could be guaranteed an extra portion of spaghetti, and the Vino was flowing freely for weeks after July 11th.

The reason is obvious. Italy are reigning champions of the World, having beaten West Germany 3-1 in a 45 minute final, which had everything concentrated into its second-half following a boring first period.

Those boisterous German's were somewhat subdued in the weeks which followed, despite a cheering recovery against France which had them singing into the early hours from the Costa del Sol, to the coast of Brittany.

That Final on Sunday, July 11th ended a month of televised football from Spain during which we thrilled at the skills of the Brazilians, groaned at the efforts of some East European sides, and hoped for success from the Home nations.

It was little Northern Ireland who provided most of the excitement for us, after Scotland had failed in what was always looked upon as the most difficult of the qualifying groups.

Ireland's performances captured the hearts of everyone following the World Cup on television, and in Belfast there were celebrations well into the early hours after Billy Bingham's team beat host nation Spain to win their group ahead of Yugoslavia, Honduras and the Spaniards.

Scotland were in fact the only British team not to qualify for the second stage, with the Irish and England carrying the flag into the next groupings.

The Scots found Brazil and Russia, formidable opposition despite getting off to a good start by beating New Zealand 5-2.

Hot favourites Brazil blasted the Scots 4-1, after beating the Russians 2-1 in their first game, and after Russia beat the New Zealanders 3-0, it was a crucial clash when Jock Stein's side met the men from behind the Iron Curtain.

It ended in a 2-2 scoreline after a tragic mistake in the Scottish defence, and the fans from North of the Border who had flooded to Spain, found themselves faced with a long journey home when their favourites went out on goal difference. Those two goals conceded against New Zealand, proved so costly.

England were favourably placed after a tremendous start to the competition. They beat France 3-1 with Bryan Robson scoring the fastest goal in the World Cup when he shot England ahead after only 27 seconds.

Victory over Czechoslovakia put England into the second phase, and a third game against Kuwait was a formality although Trevor Francis did thrill the patient 35,000 crowd who had gone to Bilbao to see a rout, with a great solo goal.

Attention turned to the second groupings, with Poland, Russia and Belgium facing each other, and Brazil, Italy and Argentina prepared for a tough passage towards the semi finals.

CUP '82

England v. Czechoslovakia. Trevor Francis

England v. Kuwait.

England v. France.

Northern Ireland were placed alongside France and Austria, while England faced Spain, and old rivals West Germany.

It looked possible that England would qualify for the semi-final stage when West Germany beat Spain 2-1 in their quarter final group game. Ron Greenwood knew that his side needed a 2-0 win over the sad Spaniards to go through, and that at the expense of a frustrating West German side which had been beaten by Algeria in the shock of Group Two.

But it was "Adios England" when, on Monday, July 5th, Greenwood's last game as England manager ended in a 0-0 draw and the German's had escaped.

However, if the England exit was sad, the Irish was a tragedy.

With a side made up of players from lesser-known, and lower division clubs, they drew 2-2 with Austria, only to come up against a French side which was to become everybody's favourite a few days later.

Ireland went out 4-1, and the scene for the semi-finals was set. Poland would meet Italy, who had stunned everyone by beating both Argentina and Brazil. Yes, Brazil full of everthing good in football, were on their way home again after a game worthy of any final.

In the other semi-final West Germany met France, and it was the blue-shirted Frenchmen who seemed to have the affair sewn-up in extra time after a thrilling 90 minutes.

They led 3-1, yet West Germany came back, and in the end it was 3-3, and a penalty shoot-out, saw the slightly lucky Germans go through.

So came the final, and it was a missed penalty which gave Italian supporters a case of severe shock when Cabrini scuffed the ground as he took the kick.

Was this to be another story of a great German escape? ITV's panel back in London felt that it might be, although Jimmy Greaves had fancied the Italians right through the competition. When they set the game on fire in the second half to take a 3-0 lead Jimmy glowed with delight.

A consolation goal saved West Germany from being the first nation **not** to score in a World Cup Final, but it was panelist Jack Charlton who summed up the competition: "I don't think we've learned a lot from what we've seen. This has been the 'Falling over World Cup'. Players have been throwing themselves all over the place at the slightest touch. Then they look around and see what's happened after they've gone down. We can do without that sort of thing in our football."

So if you thought that the beaches were a little less noisy this summer, and your bowl of minestrone was over-flowing, now you know why! Italy are champions!

GROUP TABLES

Group One:

Italy	0	Poland	0
Peru	0	Cameroon	0
Italy	1	Peru	1
Poland	0	Cameroon	0
Peru	1	Poland	5
Italy	1	Cameroon	1

	P	W	D	L	F	A	Pts
Poland	3	1	2	0	5	1	4
Italy	3	0	3	0	2	2	3
Cameroon	3	0	3	0	1	1	3
Peru	3	0	2	1	2	6	2

Group Two:

West Germany	1	Algeria	2
Chile	0	Austria	1
West Germany	4	Chile	1
Algeria	0	Austria	2
Algeria	3	Chile	2
West Germany	1	Austria	0

	P	W	D	L	F	A	Pts
West Germany	3	2	0	1	6	3	4
Austria	3	2	0	1	3	1	4
Algeria	3	2	0	1	5	5	4
Chile	3	0	0	3	3	8	0

Group Three:

Argentina	0	Belgium	1
Hungary	10	El Salvador	1
Argentina	4	Hungary	1
Belgium	1	El Salvador	0
Belgium	1	Hungary	1
Argentina	2	El Salvador	0

	P	W	D	L	F	A	Pts
Belgium	3	2	1	0	3	1	5
Argentina	3	2	0	1	6	2	4
Hungary	3	1	1	1	12	6	3
El Salvador	3	0	0	3	1	13	0

Group Four:

England	3	France	1
Czechoslovakia	1	Kuwait	1
England	2	Czechoslovakia	0
France	4	Kuwait	1
France	1	Czechoslovakia	1
England	1	Kuwait	0

	P	W	D	L	F	A	Pts
England	3	3	0	0	6	1	6
France	3	1	1	1	6	5	3
Czecho-slovakia	3	0	2	1	2	4	2
Kuwait	3	0	1	2	2	6	0

Group Five:

Spain	1	Honduras	1
Yugoslavia	0	N. Ireland	0
Spain	2	Yugoslavia	1
Honduras	1	N. Ireland	1
Honduras	0	Yugoslavia	1
Spain	0	N. Ireland	1

	P	W	D	L	F	A	Pts
N. Ireland	3	1	2	0	2	1	4
Spain	3	1	1	1	3	3	3
Yugoslavia	3	1	1	1	2	2	3
Honduras	3	0	2	1	2	3	2

Group Six:

Brazil	2	Russia	1
Scotland	5	New Zealand	2
Brazil	4	Scotland	1
Russia	3	New Zealand	0
Russia	2	Scotland	2
Brazil	4	New Zealand	0

	P	W	D	L	F	A	Pts
Brazil	3	3	0	0	10	2	6
Russia	3	1	1	1	6	4	3
Scotland	3	1	1	1	8	8	3
New Zealand	3	0	0	3	2	12	0

Group A

Poland	3	Belgium	0
Russia	1	Belgium	0
Poland	0	Russia	0

	P	W	D	L	F	A	Pts
Poland	2	1	1	0	3	0	3
Russia	2	1	1	0	1	0	3
Belgium	2	0	0	2	0	4	0

Group B

West Germany	0	England	0
Spain	1	West Germany	2
Spain	0	England	0

	P	W	D	L	F	A	Pts
W. Germany	2	1	1	0	2	1	3
England	2	0	2	0	0	0	2
Spain	2	0	1	1	1	2	1

Group C

Italy	2	Argentina	1
Brazil	3	Argentina	1
Brazil	2	Italy	3

	P	W	D	L	F	A	Pts
Italy	2	2	0	0	5	3	4
Brazil	2	1	0	1	5	4	2
Argentina	2	0	0	2	2	5	0

Group D

Austria	0	France	1
N. Ireland	2	Austria	2
N. Ireland	1	France	4

	P	W	D	L	F	A	Pts
France	2	2	0	0	5	1	4
Austria	2	0	1	1	2	3	1
N. Ireland	2	0	1	1	3	6	1

Semi-finals:

Italy Rossi 2	2	Poland	0

After extra-time:

West Germany Littbarski Rummenigge Fischer	3	**France** Platini (pen) Tresor Giresse	3

West Germany won 5-4 on penalties

Third Place Play-off:

Poland Szarmach Majewski Kupcewicz	3	**France** Girard Couriol	2

Half-time 2-1, Att. 25,000

Final:

Bernabeu Stadium, Madrid, Sunday July 11th 1982

Italy Rossi Tardelli Altobelli	3	**W. Germany** Breitner	1

Half-time 0-0, Att. 90,000

The Teams

Italy:
Zoff; Bergomi, Cabrini, Collovati, Scirea, Gentile, Oriali, Tardelli, Conti, Graziani, Rossi.
Substitutes: Altobelli for Graziani (8 min), Causio for Altobelli (85 min).

West Germany:
Schumacher, Kaltz, Forster (K.H.), Stielike, Forster (B.), Breitner, Dremmler, Littbarski, Briegel, Fischer, Rummenigge.
Substitutes: Hrubesch for Dremmler (68 min), Muller for Rummenigge (70 min).
Referee: A. Coelho (Brazil).

SNOOKERED!

Steve's Mayday Mauling

There are many reasons to remember Saturday, May 1st, 1982. That was the day when news came through of Britain's bombardment of the Falkland Island intruders; when rioting marred the start of the Arsenal-West Ham game at Highbury, and when two rugby finals ended all square.

It was on May 1st, 1982 that Widnes and Hull K.R. fought to a stalemate at Wembley in the Rugby League Challenge Cup Final, while Moseley and Gloucester shared the John Player Cup in the Twickenham final.

But for snooker star Steve Davis, it was a May Day to remember for a very different reason, as it marked perhaps his biggest defeat as a top line professional...10-1 at the hands of an unknown from Bolton, Tony Knowles.

Steve made a quick exit from the Embassy World Professional Snooker Championship before a stunned audience at Sheffield's Crucible Theatre, a far cry from the day when Steve made ITV history by becoming the first player to score 147—snooker's maximum—in a televised tournament.

A new angle on Terry Griffiths.

The day to remember was in the Lada Championship in Oldham, the morning to forget was 40 miles away across the Pennines.

The young Londoner found himself out of the top tournament after going into his game with Knowles as firm favourite to stay World Champion.

"Things like that help you to keep your feet on the ground," said Steve after defeat. "I have always felt that I have the ability to succeed, and I know I have the confidence, but you must not let it run away with you. You have to stay on top, and to stay on top you have to work hard. To lose an important game makes you realise that you have to keep on working at it."

The Davis road to success may have had to face a detour at Sheffield, but it continues to take the likeable young man on to even greater glories.

"I want to be the most successful player who ever lived. To be the greatest," he says. "I have time on my side, I am young enough to have a short successful career. I will be quite happy to retire at 34 or 35 while I am hopefully still at the top."

John Spencer (left) and Ray Reardon pose for the camera before a vital clash.

According to reports Davis could retire now. Since he turned professional just after his 21st birthday, he is alleged to have earned more money than any other British sportsman.

In tournament after tournament he established himself as virtually unbeatable. Appearance money, and exhibition invitations took him into the Super Tax bracket and he found himself in demand from the media handling television and radio interviews with as much ease and confidence as he wields a cue.

"In one interview I was asked if I felt that I was bad for snooker," says Steve. "What the interviewer meant was if I kept on winning every time I played would I turn people away from the game. What was the point of taking up snooker if you knew you had to beat Steve Davis at the end of it all?

"He compared me with Bjorn Borg... and while I feel very flattered I think my success can have the opposite effect.

"If youngsters see someone not too far in front of them in years, doing as well as I have been, then they want a share. They take up the sport and have a go, if they had to wait until they were in their thirties before they had a chance of success they might not bother," he added.

So Steve Davis is good for snooker, and while he is almost unbeatable there is always likely to be a Tony Knowles waiting in the wings to spring a surprise—and that is good for everybody, including Steve Davis.

The entourage which follows a major road race is a spectacle in itself. Here service vehicles keep a watchful eye on their riders in the Milk Race.

Take Your Time to be a TOP TOUR STAR says Phil Ligget

So you would like to be a professional cyclist and one day win the Tour de France? Well that is not an unusual dream for a youngster standing nose-pressed against a bike shop window, or pulling away the Christmas wrappings mum and dad had managed to drape around the shining, fifteen-geared velocipede currently blessing the front room.

But for the millions who dream, only a handful reach the standard required to be a top level cyclist, and this is hardly surprising.

"One of the problems," says World of Sport Cycling Commentator Phil Liggett, "is that few youngsters realise what lies ahead if they want to be a pro cyclist."

Westerdale in North Yorkshire makes a spectacular setting for competitors in the Milk Race, Britain's longest running bike race which celebrated its silver jubilee in 1982.

"To begin with they try to do too much right away, belting around everywhere at top speed, not realising that cycling in the early years should all be about building up stamina. Instead of racing around they should enjoy their sport, get out into the countryside and look around. See if they can make that hill in the distance, and find out what lies on the other side. Distance should be their aim, and not speed, that will come later."

Phil says that top cyclists hit their peak at around 26 years of age, with most professionals expecting a life span of about eight or nine years in the saddle.

A professional road race rider in Europe can expect to clock up 30,000 miles a year in training and actual events, plus a further 50,000 miles driving and travelling to races.

"It is a very hard life, and one of great dedication. I don't think there has ever been a world champion who has been born with a dream of reaching the top. World champions are made out of years of preparation, and a will to win.

"The Belgians have a saying that the rider who suffers ten minutes longer than the rest will win the race. What this means is that in an event like the Tour de France, when riders cover 2,500 of the hardest miles in cycling, everyone has to suffer. If you can cope with the pain, the tiredness and the conditions, better than everyone else, then you can be a winner."

Cycling is one of the most popular pastimes in this country, yet we have produced very few professional road racing stars.

Recognise the young chap with the microphone? It is disc jockey Jimmy Savile in his days as a cycling commentator. Jimmy actually raced at one time, and began broadcasting as announcer at Reg Harris's stadium in Manchester.

"A few years ago the late Tommy Simpson made Tour de France history by becoming the first Englishman to wear the famous leader's yellow jersey, but I feel that an English speaking rider will soon emerge, and I would not be surprised if we saw an English speaking winner of the Tour de France in the next few years," claims Phil.

"In 1981 Phil Anderson led the race for a week, and while he has been brought up in Australia, he was born in London. Stephen Roache from Dublin, winner of the Paris-Nice road race in his first year as a professional, and Sean Kelly the 1982 winner, are making the Irish challenge; and watch out for Greg Lemond the American junior world champion. He will come through as a top tour rider soon."

Perhaps there is no other sport to compare with cycling.

It requires the strength of a speed skater—in fact Eric Heiden, the man who took five gold medals in the 1980 Olympics at every distance from 500 metres to 10,000 metres, is now a professional cyclist—and the nerve of a downhill skier.

"Riders have to be prepared to cover the distance of five marathons in a day, to stay in the saddle for five hours without a break, to race against the clock as well as against opponents, and to climb mountain roads fifteen miles high, then plunge down the other side," says Phil.

So if you still have dreams of becoming a top professional cyclist remember, it is hard work, but the glory at the end of it all is well worth it.

JOCKEY QUIZ

"They're Off!" a familiar scene at a top race meeting as the gates open — but with no commentator to help, can you identify the jockey in the centre? You will find the answer on page 60.

THE LIVERPOOL SECRET

is Kept in the Cupboard

WORLD OF SPORT

Listen, do you want to know a secret? At last it can be revealed, the walls of security have been breached, and the secret of Liverpool's success discovered.

For two decades, since the great Bill Shankly took Liverpool back into the First Division, to dominate British and European soccer, rivals have tried to crack the formula of the Scousers' success.

Now that secret is out...or at least World of Sport has managed to infiltrate into the operations room at Anfield, the room where pre-match planning takes place. This is the heart of Liverpool, the machine room where patterns of play are discussed, where Bob Paisley and his backroom boys discuss the opposition, and decide on the final line-up before each game.

Nothing unusual in this, you might think, why not have a hideaway planning centre, its walls lined with tactical formulae, with tried and tested patterns of play. Why not have files on the opposition players, computerised filing and video play backs of previous games at the touch of a button...? Well, that might be all right for James Bond, but not for Liverpool.

No, their planning room is a boot cupboard!

Deep beneath the main grand-stand at Anfield, the boot room has been Liverpool's conference centre after training for many years: "It's there where we go over our plans, and chat about the opposition," says manager Bob Paisley, "it has become a bit of a tradition to have a talk in there, away from the general hurly-burly of the general atmosphere at the club.

Which team won two cups at the same time in 1982? Liverpool pick up the League Cup and the new Milk Cup after their final against Tottenham Hotspur.

Liverpool's tactical talks have paid vast dividends since the early days under the late Bill Shankly, when he arrived from Huddersfield, with one aim...to lift Liverpool from the Second Division, something hard to believe nowadays with Anfield's record showing more success each year.

In twenty years Liverpool have only looked ahead, and after the building of Shankly, moved on with the guile of Paisley to earn Europe's top soccer crown three times.

The name "Liverpool" is being engraved on the League Championship trophy with almost monotonous regularity, and the club seems capable of continuing their success for at least the next five years.

"We plan ahead," says Bob Paisley, "and we are always able to prepare for the day when someone has to step down. By forward thinking we fill the gaps before they occur."

It was Bill Shankly who brought players like Ron Yeats, and Ian St John to Anfield as he built the first great side. Then there was the Liverpool generation which included John Toshack and Kevin Keegan.

Ray Clemence bridged a gap between one side and the next, as Kenny Dalglish and Phil Thompson took Liverpool into the '80's, and now the names of Ian Rush and Ronnie Whelan have joined the Anfield greats.

Who will be next, only time will reveal, but one thing can be certain, once the backroom boys start to talk about them in the Anfield boot cupboard they are on their way to glory...and that is no secret!

WORLD OF SPORT

Step by step to victory for Liverpool as Ronnie Whelan scores one of his two vital Wembley goals in the League Cup Final.

One cup well worth winning—delight shows on Phil Thompson's face after he picks up the European Cup for Liverpool.

MARATHON MANIA

Despite the fact that there were 106 mass marathons held in Britain in 1982, the mania for running the 26 mile 385 yard gruelling race has not reached its peak. Marathon running will be with us for some time yet, and while some of the smaller events may die out, the big races are here to stay.

That is the opinion of World of Sport running expert Tom McNab, writer and authority on what has now become the biggest participation sport in the western world.

Up to a few years ago angling held first place in the popularity poll in this country, with sports like darts and walking fighting it out in second and third places. But then came the American jogging boom of the Seventies, and this was followed closely by the marathon. Suddenly running was big business.

"It is quite astonishing really, a few years ago running shoe companies could expect to sell maybe 50,000 pairs of shoes in a good year. Nowadays it is more like 5,000,000, with runners thinking nothing of spending £40 for a pair of good, reliable, purpose-built shoes," says Tom.

Runners in the Pony British marathon leave the start for a hilly run around Bolton.

The marathon bug was created out of the American jogging cult. Suddenly joggers, who had enjoyed their plod around the park, felt that they needed a target. New York's Fred Lebow decided that his New York Running Club would organise a mass marathon, and the world suddenly found that the target had been provided.

The joggernauts prepared for a mass assault on the 26 mile course, and in 1980 over 7,500 competitors set out through the streets of New York under the watchful eye of the television camera.

"Actually television played a massive part in the rise in popularity of running. Suddenly the man in the street saw someone performing on television who was comparable with himself," says Tom. "The super athletes were the untouchables, it was no use trying to compete with the Coe's and Ovett's because they were in another class. But here they saw people like themselves, flogging themselves for three or four hours, and even longer in some cases, to complete the course."

The marathon took on a new form. Until 1980 it had been the hardest race in athletics. Few will forget the achievements of past marathon runners in the Olympic Games, the glory when great men crossed the finishing line, forcing their tired legs into an extra stride, many will remember moments of sadness like the collapse of British star Jim Peters so near the finish of a heat-baked run.

Now completing a marathon was as important as winning one.

The mass events became two races in one, and the boom was bound to reach Britain.

Through Manchester city centre runners stretch for as far as the eye can see. Competitors in the Manchester Charity Marathon raised over £1 million for hundreds of organisations.

In 1981 London staged its first mass run, with figures similar to the first New York field. Other events followed, like two races in Greater Manchester which together attracted 15,000 runners, one of them—the 1981 Manchester Charity Marathon producing the fastest time by a Briton in this country that year in Steve Kenyon's 2hrs 11mins 54secs.

The growth continued. Dublin, Birmingham, Sheffield, Stoke-on-Trent all became venues for mass runs, then in October 1981, New York broke all records with a field of 17,000 starters.

The battle was on for the biggest field, even though the race promoters claimed that perhaps this was not the true aim of the mass event.

London found itself over-subscribed with an embarrassing 18,000 entrants in May 1982, while Manchester decided that it would try a new idea and ran the 10,000 field Piccadilly Radio Charity Marathon on a Saturday evening.

Altogether 106 mass marathons were registered by the Amateur Athletics Association in 1982, meaning that somewhere in the region of 200,000 people set out to run over 26 miles. But why?

"A lot of runners simply do it because they feel that they want to achieve something," says Tom McNab, "once they got the bug they wanted to keep on running. Once they had an objective, they had to run a marathon."

"Some people took up running because they saw it as a way of losing excess weight. Surprisingly people with what you could call "bad athletic records", suddenly found themselves at 40, achieving what they couldn't achieve at 20. Smokers who puffed away at 30 to 40 cigarettes a day, found that they could cut down because of their running, because by cutting down they could run better. They changed their eating and drinking habits, and found that they were losing weight, and feeling better for it," says Tom.

"Their lives were being transformed because of running, and preparing for a marathon brought about a permanent change for many people. Once they realised how good they felt because of their fitness they did not want to slip back into their old ways," he added.

But with so many marathons will the day not arrive when runners have had too much of a good thing?

"I don't think so, and neither do my friends who are running experts," he says, "we feel that the peak has not yet been reached. And when that day comes, while a certain percentage of runners will drop out, they will be replaced by others equally keen to take part. Runners getting ready for marathon competition will cover around 1,500 miles in a year. Anyone doing that sort of running is going to feel all the better for it, and no-one wants to give up something which is keeping them healthy."

So the boom continues, marathon mania is with us for some time yet, and if you want to get fit the best way seems to be to run for it...if you can't beat them...join them!

CLIMB THE LADDER

WORLD OF SPORT

Try your sporting skills on this upside down quiz. The easier questions are at the foot of the ladder...the more you answer the higher you climb – only the sporting super-brains will reach the top, but if you need a shove you will find the answers on page 60!

Step thirteen:
Can you name this famous partnership of the turf?

Step twelve:
What is the exact distance of a marathon?

Step eleven:
Who was named 1982 Football Manager of the Year?

Step ten:
Can you name this international star?

Step nine:
Who is the Golden Bear?

Step eight:
Where was Glenn Turner Born? South Africa, Australia, or New Zealand?

Step seven: Who holds the Jules Rimet Trophy?

Step Six:
Another Scot to spot...who is it?

Step five:
Who won the Scottish Cup in 1982?

Step four:
What is the maximum break possible in snooker?

Step three:
Name this sporting star?

Step two:
Jayne Torville and Christopher ––––?

Step one:
Who scored Aston Villa's goal in the European Cup Final?

CRAZY CAPTIONS

WORLD OF SPORT

The camera closes in. The all seeing eye of television brings a close-up of a world sporting star into our living rooms. Just what is he thinking? What is he saying at this crucial moment? That is when the commentator has an important role to play, using his imagination to add more excitement to the scene.

Here our commentators go beyond the normal call of duty to capture the excitement, and bring you the tension!

Perhaps this is not really what is happening here—but it does raise a smile.

Top *"And Botham seems to be in extreme pain. Once again he has stopped beside the umpire, and he's bringing his arm over slowly and pointing out the troublesome spot just below his chest. Not surprisingly he's been bowling with the wind all morning."*

Bottom *"McDermott is certainly out on his own, and with the rest of the Liverpool team, and most of the spectators having a half time cup of tea, it looks as if we'll have quite a wait for this corner..."*

Top

"And as the players were changing over a few moments ago I noticed Connors slipping something into McEnroe's barley-water. Probably nothing... but wait... what's happening now! It's obviously having some sort of effect, and the crowd love it!"

Bottom

"And just before this round Trevino was telling me that if he failed to get into the prize money he would not only eat his hat, but his clubs as well. And it seems as though he's starting... that looks like a sand-wedge to me!"

WITH WHEELS SPINNING

The engine roars into top revs, the car lurches on the stone covered pathway, its rear end swinging from side to side as the driver fights with the wheel. He keeps the car under control as it nears a tight left hand bend, allowing it to slide into the centre of the track before he accelerates through the hazard.

On either side of the track crowds of enthusiasts clad in waterproof clothing, gumboots and wrapped against the cold, pad out their applause in gloved hands.

This is what rallying is all about, and why Britain's Lombard RAC Rally has such a fascinating appeal for lovers of motor sport.

The Lombard RAC, Britain's top rally, is compressed into just four days, during which the contestants, and their cars, have to cover 1,817 gruelling miles in England, Wales and Scotland, with 66 special stages stretching over 464 miles of testing driving.

Jim Porter who is deputy clerk to the rally course, says he tries to make the route as tough and demanding as possible, "Because that is what the top drivers want. We want the Lombard RAC Rally to be the one they all want to win, and we have to make it as difficult, yet as fair as we can."

They turn out in their thousands to cram onto hillsides, line forest pathways, and fill tourist spots like Trentham Gardens and Knowsley Safari Park to watch the skills of the drivers and hear the roar of their engines, rather than the roar of the wild animals normally associated with places like the latter.

That means that Jim and his colleagues are working on the event well in advance of its late November schedule.

"We start on the next one even before the present rally has finished," he says.

Of the many classes of motor sport, rallying is perhaps the one which appeals most of all to the man in the street.

In events like the Lombard RAC he can see vehicles not too different from his own family saloon, and while there is a difference, he can make favourable comparisons with his own driving and the skills of the experts.

"Mind you, competitors have to travel from one special stage to another on normal roads, and observe the traffic laws, and speed limit, just like anyone else," says Jim Porter. "But once the flag goes down at the start of a stage you can see the difference."

The crowds who watch the Lombard RAC are almost as amazing as the

drivers. Last year over 400,000 turned out to view the Sunday driving in Weston Park, near Telford; Sutton Park, in the centre of Birmingham; Donington Park; Trentham Gardens near Stoke-on-Trent, and at Knowsley Safari Park near Liverpool.

They are as enthusiastic as their counterparts in speedway, moto-cross, and circuit racing, although the rally fans do sometimes have to make the best of a bad lot when it comes to weather, and conditions underfoot.

Covering the event for television can have its problems too, not only do camera positions have to be found which show the most difficult and spectacular sections of special stages, but there is the safety angle to be considered all the time. No cameraman wants to find himself on the receiving end of a ton of high speed steel as it hops off a Welsh mountain at 120 miles an hour—and who can blame him!

Because it is part of the Rally World Championship, the Lombard RAC is established as a major event in the motor sport calendar, but it was far from this way in its early days.

When Timo Makinen won the first Lombard RAC in 1974—the RAC had established the event before other sponsors were found to cover overheads—the only rally of any significance was the Monte Carlo, but Basil Tye, managing director of the RAC Motor Sport Association says: "Television helped to change all that, and rallying has become a popular sport both on and off our screens. Our aim over the years has been to improve the rally, and make it more enjoyable and more varied for competitors and spectators".

The organisers would seem to have succeeded, but overheads are constantly on the increase—in 1981 the RAC had to pay £45,000 to the Forestry Commission to use the forestry tracks, a cost of 70p for every mile covered by the 150 cars.

Behind the Scenes at MANCHESTER UNITED

The last fan has gone home. The floodlights have been switched off, and the groundman locks the door on another game. To many people this is a typical scene on a Saturday evening during an English winter, as the football ground is locked up for the weekend – next game, a reserve fixture in a week's time.

But that is a scene from the past. Nowadays clubs have begun to realise that football is with us for seven days every week, and for 52 weeks a year.

The season may end in May, but the club goes on. The game might finish at 4.40 p.m. on a Saturday afternoon, but the final whistle never blows.

One of the first clubs to realise this was Manchester United, trend-setters of the 50's and 60's, who have moved into the 80's with a super stadium ringed with executive seating, and with facilities within their complex to ensure that there is a cash flow at Old Trafford every day of the year.

The World Cup in 1966 saw the first steps taken towards the super-stadium Old Trafford has become today. Then, as one of the group venues for the games played in the north, it was modernised, largely through the building of a cantilever stand fronting a row of private boxes.

The super fan was arriving together with the super-stadium.

Food from the giant kitchens is served to diners in Manchester United's Executive Suite. The Grill Room and Europa Suite have their own cooking facilities.

The indoor training area at The Cliff provides round-the-year facilities for Manchester United's players, while Old Trafford gets an end-of-season facelift. All was ready for the sprinkler system to water the new turf at the start of another season.

Today those boxes have been extended to run in an "L" down one side of the ground and around behind the goal at the scoreboard end of Old Trafford.

Other executive seating is also provided for members of the elite club which provides five-star cuisine for supporters before a home game, and for anyone who wishes to use it on any other day of the week.

Training facilities at United include an indoor pitch which ensures that there is always somewhere to kick a football even in the worst winters. The practice ground also houses a fully equipped gymnasium, sauna, and physio room, as well as a playing area complete with covered accommodation where the fans watch Saturday morning junior games.

Like so many clubs Manchester United were aware that there would be a financial change in the face of football as we entered the 1980's, and added a lottery to the already thriving Development Association competitions launched to improve facilities at Old Trafford.

The Executive Suite, and Grill Room — a steak bar below the luxury restaurant — was joined by the Europa Suite, as ground development grew, and now Old Trafford can stage a large dinner, a giant conference, and several business meetings all on the same day.

With United retaining their title of the top supported League club in 1981-82, the backroom staff have also shown that they are top of their own league in providing the best off-the-field facilities for their customers.

"CUP FINAL QUOTES"

World of Sport's football experts went into extra time themselves to cover the 1982 F.A. Cup Final. Here are some of the things they had to say during the two matches.

Jack Charlton: The first half has passed quickly, and that's usually the sign that it's a good game. But one thing that has to be looked at...everytime Spurs have had a shot at goal, and the 'keeper has made some good saves, Archibald keeps getting in offside positions, and the linesman ignores him. If he gets one it's going to be unfair. All in all, Spurs have had the most shots but the two most dangerous situations for me have both come from QPR.

Brain Clough: Those Tottenham legs look a bit tired. They've had a lot of games, taken a lot of kicks, and run a lot of miles this season. They would have liked to have gone in at half time with a cushion of a goal, they know now they've got it all to do.

Glenn Hoddle: Football's all about playing to the final whistle and we let ourselves down at the end. When I scored our goal I thought I had knocked the ball too far on the greasy surface, but I just hit it and next time I saw it, it was in the back of the net.

Peter Hucker: It was one of the most exciting ends to a final for a long time. I think it died off a bit in the second half, both teams were a bit wary of each other, but in extra time I thought it was a marvellous final, and a great finish.

Steve Perryman: Obviously we're very disappointed that we've come off the field level, after being a goal up and so very few minutes to go. But we'll pick ourselves up and come back here on Thursday and win it.

Tony Currie: One down with seven minutes to go it's pretty obvious that you've got to roll your sleeves up and do your best. They had a lot of play in the first half and we had the best of the second.

Jack Charlton: I thought that the goal Tottenham scored had won the game for them, and if they had carried on going forward instead of messing about they would have won it. Instead they gave away the corner and QPR equalised.

Ian St John: QPR are getting another bite of the cherry, and they deserve it. They only had four corners in the game and every time they got one you thought something might happen. Spurs felt that the game was finished, and they started messing around, a lot of sloppy play. They gave away the corner and got punished for it, so I say well done Rangers.

Ian St John: I feel really sorry for them tonight. They played so well. After losing the early goal they really deserved to win. In the second half they had lots of crosses going in, with Spurs hanging on. You've got to give them credit.

Jimmy Greaves: When it's not going for you, when the man in the clouds is not on your side, there's not much you can do about it, and while one can say that Spurs were a bit lucky, we have to give them a bit of credit, it has been a long hard season for them. They looked tired, they looked jaded, and Rangers went at them and did everything they possibly could.

Brian Clough: When Tottenham came out to look at the pitch Glenn Hoddle was first, and I've got a feeling he's going to run the match tonight. He looks in good nick, and if he's prepared himself since Saturday and used the break he's had to rest and to contemplate, and prepare himself for tonight, I think he can genuinely show his true form and run this match.
(Later)...How wrong can you be!

Tottenham Hotspur — Kings of Wembley. That is a title Spurs can proudly claim after playing "four" F.A. Cup Finals in a year, and winning the Cup twice.

After drawing with Manchester City in 1981, Spurs picked up the trophy through a mid-week replay. In 1982 it was the same story, this time Queen's Park Rangers were runners-up.

England's Tony Morley and Glenn Hoddle try out a new mode of transport — at least it would be one way of avoiding traffic jams.

Stand by for the ICE-HOCKEY BOOM

WORLD OF SPORT

With darts continuing to prosper, and speedway bound to hold its fans, the predicted growth of ice-hockey is not only going to bring us more excitement on television... it's going to make Dave Lanning a very busy man indeed!

Dave Lanning reckons you can play darts in the garage, but former World Champion John Lowe prefers the comfort of his study. And just look at those trophies.

If past records are anything to go by we are about to have a television boom in ice-hockey.

The man who claims this is World of Sport commentator Dave Lanning, and Dave puts his claim down to this: "In the 60's I was involved in the big increase in popularity of speedway, a sport which is still well supported today. Then came the growth of darts as a television sport, and I was caught up in that too. My latest mission has been to cover ice-hockey, and I can certainly feel that there is a growth in this sport as well."

Dave sees ice-hockey as perfect for the armchair fan.

"It has excitement, is always moving and full of incidents. There is always something to look at and talk about, in fact there are so many changes and substitutions it's actually a bit of a nightmare for commentators. No sooner have you got used to one set of players and their numbers, than there has been a switch and you have a new group to identify," he says.

America's World Speedway Champion Bruce Penhall shows his skills on a mini-bike after celebrating his Championship Victory.

But problems apart the versatile Dave Lanning is sure that he is onto a winner—and so is television if it sticks to ice-hockey.

"I was involved in the growth of speedway on television, and World of Sport were there before anyone else. Speedway fans were clamouring for coverage, and they responded magnificently to it. They told the television chiefs how much they appreciated the coverage, and everyone was happy."

Then came the dart explosion, and there is a story which circulates within London Weekend Television, that the man responsible for the rise to fame of the pub and club game was none other than soccer supremo Jimmy Hill.

One day, during Jimmy's World of Sport days, before his transfer to pastures new, he was chatting in the office with a group of colleagues: "Why don't you get some cameras over to the News of the World Darts Finals," Jimmy is alleged to have suggested. They did, and darts became a television sport.

"It is perfect for T.V.," says Dave "the cameras can bring viewers everything they want. They can see what is going on, can see how it is done, and everything happens quickly. Instant sport. That is why darts has grown into the most popular sport around."

Not only televised darts, but the game itself has grown out of all proportion in the popularity stakes. It is reckoned that around 90,000 pubs and clubs have dart boards, and 85 per cent of these establishments have teams playing in the darts leagues.

From the North of Scotland to the most westerly tip of Cornwall, people are playing darts, and the game itself has become more standardised through television.

"Once games were regionalised, certain areas played certain types of game, not always 501 up. Some areas threw from closer to the board than others, but the British Darts Organisation, and the popularity of televised darts, has brought about a form of standardisation, and the game is all the better for it."

There are other reasons for the darts boom.

Nick Faldo.

"It is cheap and easy to play," says Dave, "you can buy a very good set of darts for under £5, and hang a dart board almost anywhere, on the back of the garage door, in the garden on a tree, anywhere. And anyone can play, you don't have to be superfit, or go into training to play darts. Of course you can pay as much as £40 for a set of tungsten darts, but what a lot of people don't realise is that these arrows will last you forever. If they become your favourites you won't want to change them. There is very little follow through in the dart selling trade, once you have sold a set to someone you hardly ever see them again."

Dave defends the image of the popular dart professionals whom many claim are fat-bellied, smoke-blowing boozers, who seem to spend all their time between throwing, downing as much beer as they can.

"Sure there are one or two plump ones about, and certainly they like a drink or two," he says. "But there is nothing wrong with the game, it does not have the image of some of what we call the Olympic sports with a background of drugs, steroids, and things like preventing youngsters from reaching puberty so that they can bend their bodies over a gymnasium bar—and the image of darts will be changing slightly in the future too, the youngsters are coming through and will be making their mark on the scene soon."

NEW FACES
and some old ones too...

The ups and downs of another season saw a new face emerge in Division One, a face known well enough to some First Division clubs, yet fresh enough to create a curiosity amongst supporters and bring them back to "live" football.

Watford — Elton John's elite little outfit had risen from obscurity to soccer's pinnacle, Division One of the Football League.

"I always hoped and dreamed that one day we would get there," said perhaps the best known chairman in soccer, "and getting there is like a dream."

To the fans of Watford, Elton John had kept a promise.

Many in football raised more than the odd eyebrow when the singing star, renowned more for his outrageous spectacles than his shrewd business ability, took over at Vicarage Road as chairman.

There was no doubting his enthusiasm, he was a Watford fanatic, but he had to prove himself in the boardroom hot seat, in the same way he had convinced the music world of his ability years before. He passed that audition with flying colours. Now Division One look out!

Elton John would be first to heap praise on the part played by Watford manager Graham Taylor in the rise, and rise, of the club, and anyone doubting the endurance of Watford in the top division should look at their cup record against top opposition.

The scoreboard at Vicarage Road tells its own story. This was a memorable F.A. Cup clash for Watford . . . the next appointment was in Division One.

Division Two champions Luton set the promotion pace for most of the season. Here they are seen in action against Norwich City who also stepped up, although a massive 17 points separated first and third places.

Wigan player-manager Larry Lloyd celebrates Athletic's promotion to Division Three. Behind Larry a smiling Bobby Charlton joins in the festivities with his fellow directors at Springfield Park, while (left) chairman Freddie Pye seems to be pondering the future... Division Two perhaps?

Luton Town are another new name in Division One for 1982-83, although unlike Watford, they have been there before.

The new three point system introduced last season, saw them rise as Second Division Champions with a massive 88 points, one more than Division One winners Liverpool.

Kenilworth Road with its 23,000 capacity will be the scene of many an epic battle this season as the new boys try to establish themselves.

Other promotion candidates Sheffield Wednesday and Queens Park Rangers, had to step aside and let Norwich return to Division One, with only two points separating the three clubs.

Wednesday and Rangers can look forward to trips to Leeds, Wolves and Middlesbrough as three clubs with histories of success took the dreaded drop. Middlesbrough can comfort themselves slightly, if unconvincingly, that their 39 points was the highest total by a bottom club!

Burnley, one of the League's original members, took a step back to Division Two as Third Division Champions, giving veteran goalkeeper Alan Stevenson a testimonial season to remember. Their last championship was the Division Two trophy in 1973, and older supporters at Turf Moor still have happy memories of 1960 when the club topped Division One.

Carlisle were pipped into second place on goal difference in Division Three's title race, with Fulham third.

Cardiff, Wrexham and Orient were relegated from Division Two, while Wimbledon, Swindon, Bristol City, and Chester, fell from Division Three.

But one of the Cinderella stories of the 1981-82 season came from Springfield Park, Wigan, where under a board of directors which includes Bobby Charlton, and led by manager Larry Lloyd the former Liverpool and Forest centre half, the ex-non-leaguers were promoted.

Division Four's champions were points - crazy Sheffield United, who accumulated 96 under the new system, with Bradford City in second place, and Bournemouth fourth.

However, it was third placed Wigan, behind only on goal difference, who caught the headlines. Only four years after playing Premier League football they had put their town on the soccer map... and that, in a Rugby League area is something!

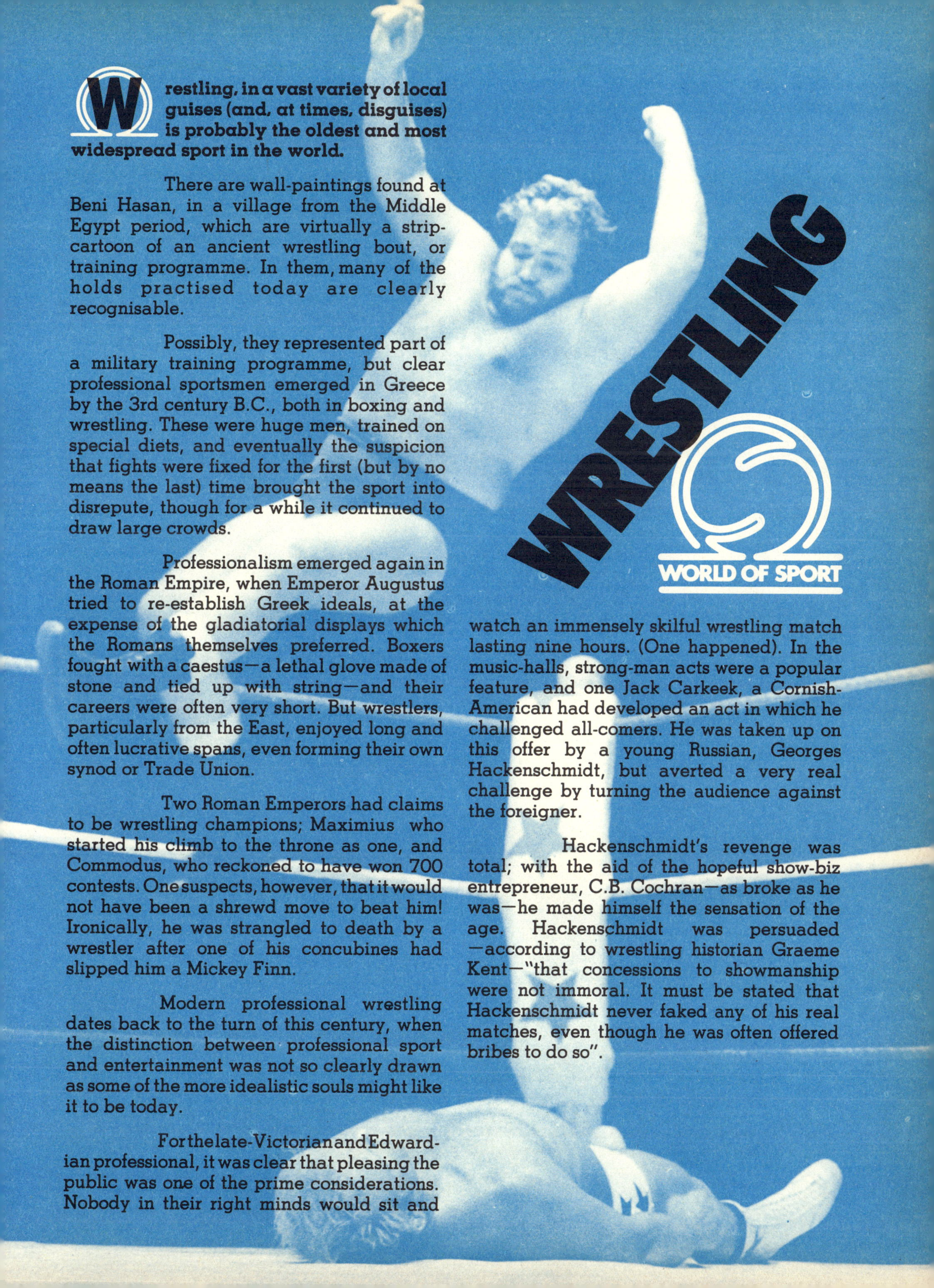

WRESTLING

Wrestling, in a vast variety of local guises (and, at times, disguises) is probably the oldest and most widespread sport in the world.

There are wall-paintings found at Beni Hasan, in a village from the Middle Egypt period, which are virtually a strip-cartoon of an ancient wrestling bout, or training programme. In them, many of the holds practised today are clearly recognisable.

Possibly, they represented part of a military training programme, but clear professional sportsmen emerged in Greece by the 3rd century B.C., both in boxing and wrestling. These were huge men, trained on special diets, and eventually the suspicion that fights were fixed for the first (but by no means the last) time brought the sport into disrepute, though for a while it continued to draw large crowds.

Professionalism emerged again in the Roman Empire, when Emperor Augustus tried to re-establish Greek ideals, at the expense of the gladiatorial displays which the Romans themselves preferred. Boxers fought with a caestus—a lethal glove made of stone and tied up with string—and their careers were often very short. But wrestlers, particularly from the East, enjoyed long and often lucrative spans, even forming their own synod or Trade Union.

Two Roman Emperors had claims to be wrestling champions; Maximius who started his climb to the throne as one, and Commodus, who reckoned to have won 700 contests. One suspects, however, that it would not have been a shrewd move to beat him! Ironically, he was strangled to death by a wrestler after one of his concubines had slipped him a Mickey Finn.

Modern professional wrestling dates back to the turn of this century, when the distinction between professional sport and entertainment was not so clearly drawn as some of the more idealistic souls might like it to be today.

For the late-Victorian and Edwardian professional, it was clear that pleasing the public was one of the prime considerations. Nobody in their right minds would sit and watch an immensely skilful wrestling match lasting nine hours. (One happened). In the music-halls, strong-man acts were a popular feature, and one Jack Carkeek, a Cornish-American had developed an act in which he challenged all-comers. He was taken up on this offer by a young Russian, Georges Hackenschmidt, but averted a very real challenge by turning the audience against the foreigner.

Hackenschmidt's revenge was total; with the aid of the hopeful show-biz entrepreneur, C.B. Cochran—as broke as he was—he made himself the sensation of the age. Hackenschmidt was persuaded—according to wrestling historian Graeme Kent—"that concessions to showmanship were not immoral. It must be stated that Hackenschmidt never faked any of his real matches, even though he was often offered bribes to do so".

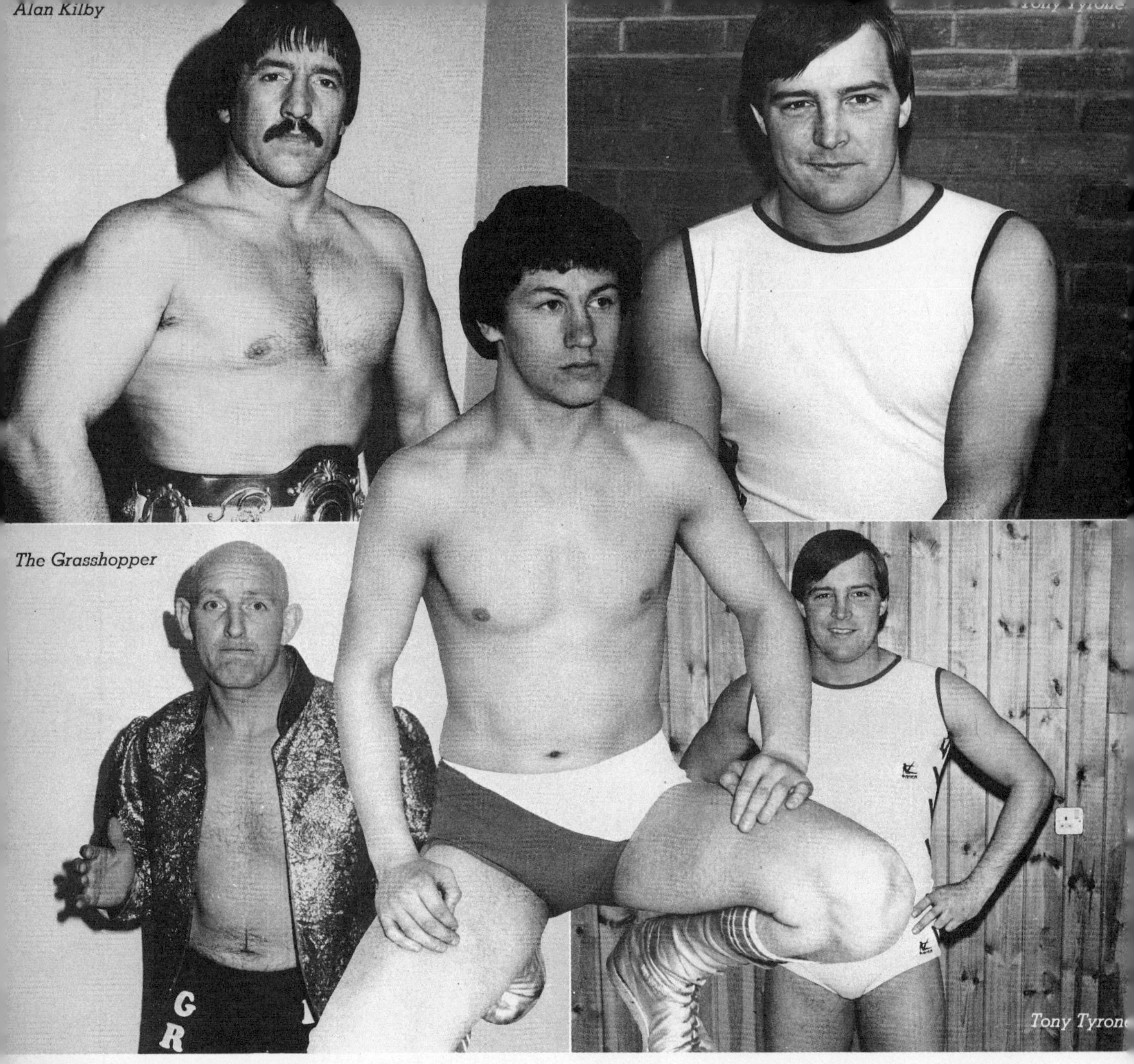

Alan Kilby

Tony Tyrone

The Grasshopper

Tony Tyrone

Everybody, as Schnoz said later, wanted to get into the act. This was the "golden age" of wrestling—as of so many sports. Possibly the Great War killed not only millions of people, but a sense of trust and enjoyment as well. What was once a showman's challenge (with the stakes in favour of the house) tended to become a rip-off. Still, serious pro wrestlers pursued their business. The Press ignored them. Those aesthetes who did not understand athletes scorned them, perhaps as clowns who entered Hengler's Circus. Still, the public was faithful; and so were the wrestlers.

The break-through for pro-wrestling in this country came with TV. The early ITV bosses wanted to produce something that was genuinely popular, which the BBC did not have. And wrestling was an immediate answer.

The chaos of minor promotions, to whom nobody could go directly, was brought into some order by the formation of Joint Promotions: ITV went to them, and they still hold the contract. This is not to disparage any others, but TV needs, above all, continuity. Then entertainment and variety; skill and personality; black and white; good and bad; possibly—as was demanded once by theatre critics "a willing suspension of disbelief".

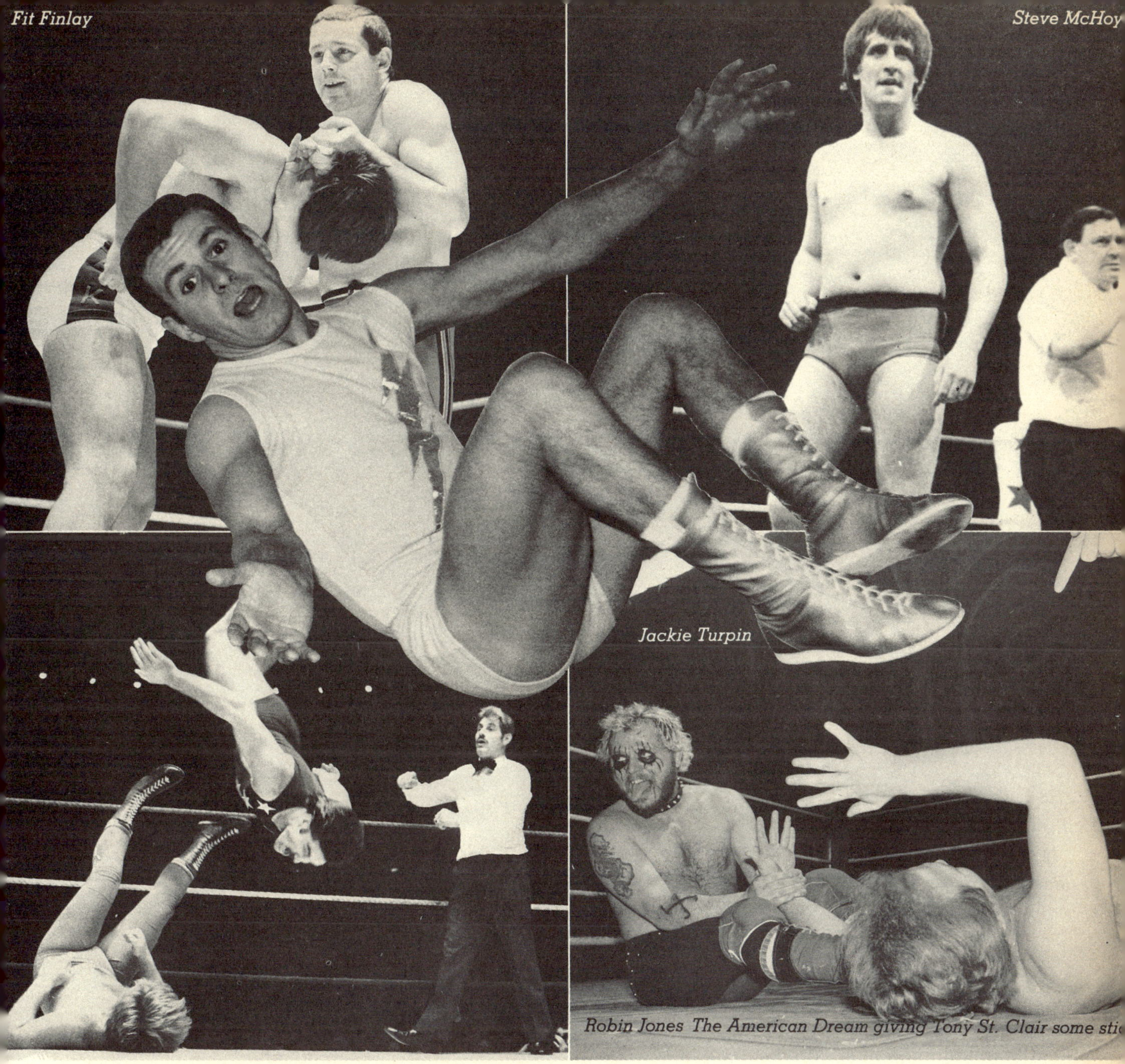

Fit Finlay

Steve McHoy

Jackie Turpin

Robin Jones The American Dream giving Tony St. Clair some sti

One man who has hung up his suspension for good (but the game is full of comebacks) is Mick McManus. A Londoner who discovered that the best way to be good was to be bad, he retired last year to concentrate on developing his sport through Dale-Martin, a major contributor to Joint Promotions.

Mick tells us that "I'll miss the crowds more than anything. Even if they thought they didn't like me, I always got satisfaction from the numbers that were there". He'll least miss the travelling. "140 venues a year—that's the average. All over the country." As for home life? "Well, if you marry a gardener, you know he's going to get sore hands".

The constant activity was mostly enough to keep Mick in good nick; but he tried to visit gyms outside town: "You get to known the YMCA's over the years". And, when in London for a few days, he tried to keep active, with weights and other measures.

His best moments were Tournaments watched by the Duke of Edinburgh and the Duke of Kent at the Albert Hall; what a marvellous venue, to hear the cheers from so high to the ringside. And the time he beat Eddie Capelli, before a London crowd, to win his first British welterweight title.

Big Daddy's grand entrance to clapping and music as his fans flock round him.

He reckons that the best technical wrestler he's seen was the Scot, George Kidd, and that "Big Daddie" (a much more media-worthy name than Shirley Crabtree—but maybe less British) represents a "John Bull type of feller" who appeals to all classes and ages. For the future, he thinks we should be looking for, among others, Steve Logan (almost a reverse image of his old tag partner), Fit Finlay, carrying an old Irish tradition into English rings and Johnny Appollon.

And, whatever the wrestlers may get up to in the ring, it's worth remembering that they, like their forebears, outside always help charities. It's a prime duty.

One wrestling fan has written a poem about those in the crowd who may cheer but can't jump around too much. The disabled. Part of it runs:

"We're wrestling with prejudice, with ignorance and fate.
We're wrestling with buildings, steps, dislike and even hate.
We grapple every day to overcome things you can do with ease.
Don't patronise, talk down to us, but lend a hand please...
WE'RE WRESTLING, TOO"

Keep on grappling.

Verse (c) Pandora 20a Verseilles Road SE 20 8AX.
Reference **A Pictorial History of Wrestling** by Graeme Kent.
Spring Books (Hamlyn) 1968.

ACTION

VILLA ~ CHAMPIONS OF EUROPE

Peter Withe after scoring the Champions Cup only goal.

Aston Villa after their win over Bayern Munich, the European Champions Cup.

Dennis Mortimer, Captain.

Aston Villa that glorious, magnificent, frustrating club is back at the top again!

Villa who have delighted and disappointed their fans within weeks — they won the League Championship in 1981 and struggled to 11th place a season later — picked out the plum prize of the European Cup when nobody gave them a chance.

Facing Bayern Munich in Rotterdam they stunned the Germans with a display of dogged British determination after losing goalkeeper Jimmy Rimmer in the ninth minute.

It was a fairytale night for stand-in Nigel Spink whose previous first team game had been away to Nottingham Forest on Boxing Day 1979!

Peter Withe scored the only goal of the game and now Villa are Kings of Europe.

The Pressure is on the BIG BOYS!

Who would be a football manager? Well according to Tommy Docherty – the man who claims to have had more clubs than Jack Nicklaus – everybody who watches the game, feels that he or SHE could make a better job than some of the big names in the game.

"There are 50,000 other managers out there on a Saturday afternoon," says The Doc "all of them could have picked a better team than you, and all of them would play in a different way, use their substitutes at a different time, and pull off anyone other than the player you decide to replace. You are on a loser — unless you are winning, then you are the greatest manager in the world. Until the next time you are behind, then they want your head."

That illustrates the kind of pressures the big boys of soccer management face. There is pressure from the fans to succeed, pressure from the directors to spend wisely, and pressure from the players who want the best that they can get out of their career.

Coventry coach Dave Sexton — who felt the cruellest blow in soccer when Manchester United parted company with him after seven successive League wins, and a reasonably good season — says "Players careers are short, and they want to make the best of them. You cannot guarantee anyone a first team place every week, but when you change a side you are the hero and the villain. The player you include thinks you are the greatest, and the one you leave out..."

Other pressures face the top managers from within the club. They have to go to the board of directors to request big sums of money needed to buy players nowadays. Money wisely spent can make their job more secure, but money which apparently has been spent with little effect,

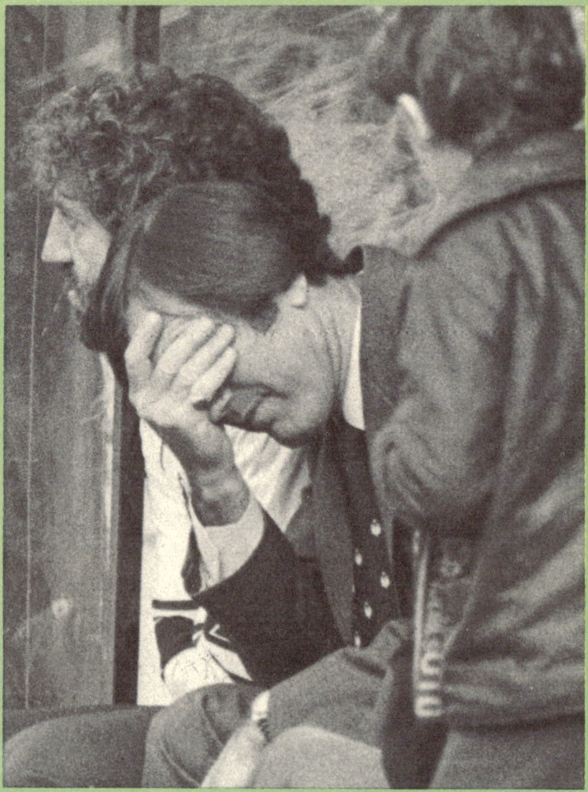

can mean that they find themselves in an embarrassing position.

"We are on a loser" says one First Division boss who prefers to remain anonymous. "The board appoint us to do a job, and when things go wrong we face the music. We can't make a mistake".

It would appear that the directors can make errors and get away with them. They appoint the manager, he fails, proving that they made the mistake in the first place, yet most boards are immune to the situation. They stay, the manager goes.

However the pressures currently on clubs will see a lot of careful administration in the future. There are likely to be many clubs facing severe financial restrictions in the mid '80s because of falling attendances, and the rising price of the game.

It is a vicious circle. Players demand higher wages; clubs have to pay higher fees for players; attendances fall because fans have either other interests, or cannot afford to watch their team regularly; admission prices increase to make ends meet — and the faithful few who can afford it, fork out for their football.

At the end of last season one Fourth Division manager said: "Another one over, and another one to look ahead to. But what will happen I don't know. There is no way that I can afford to buy new players, the wages bill is bound to increase, and we will be forced to ask the fans to pay more for their football.

"A lot of them are out of work because jobs are hard to find round here, I think that we will struggle even more next year, and could even have to go part-time. The pressure is tremendous to make money from outside the game itself, and we are just keeping our head above water."

So it would seem the pressure is on not only for the big boys, but for the minnows as well.

Now, who wants to be a football manager?

THE PFA

The supreme accolade in any profession is to be singled out for recognition by your fellow professionals". Dickie Davies' opening to this year's Professional Footballers' Association awards dinner put the star-studded evening in true perspective. These awards are the ones the professionals themselves value above all others. This has been the keynote of the acceptance speeches by every one of the nine PFA Players of the Year from Norman Hunter in 1974 to Kevin Keegan this year. And when a man who has twice won the European Footballer of the Year Trophy, as Kevin had, values the vote of his fellow pros above all others, you need no further endorsement. And that would certainly go for the winners of the Young Player of the Year too. You only need to browse through the names of some past winners to see how good the collective judgement has been. Internationals like Andy Gray, Tony Woodcock, Cyrille Regis and Glen Hoddle are all past winners.

But what attracts around 1,000 PFA members and guests to the dinner year after year, is not just the chance to honour the success stories of the year and some of the greatest names from the past who have picked up the Special Award but the fact that the lower levels of the game get their recognition too. And believe me, those Second, Third and Fourth Division players who make it into their divisional teams — also chosen by their 'peers' — value the honour (and the mementos they take home) as much as the main winners do.

So a great social and professional occasion for all levels of our national game. But it's so much more. The presence of ITV cameras has made sure of that. Late on a Sunday evening there has to be more to the mixture than pure football. Something for example to appeal to the women viewers — that's apart from the occasional hairy chests of the players who prefer evening dress worn beach-style! It can't **all** be football faces and chat, however much of a novelty it is to see players in formal (or fairly formal) dress. Hence the comedy element.

Soccer has not only bred a rich vein of front-line comedians (some might nominate the odd Manager!), but also a 'second wave' of part-timers who year after year have kept the pros on their toes. The Church is a prolific source. Remember Canon Reg Smith of Bury . . . a devout worshipper at the humble Gigg Lane shrine? "Each week we announce the crowd changes to the team!" The Vicar of Leeds was another shrewd observer. In the heydays of Don Revie's famous Leeds side, he couldn't, he admitted, resist a reference to his favourite team and to underline his point, he dedicated a hymn to Norman Hunter . . . "We plough the fields and scatter!" Bob "The Cat" Bevan, the amateur goalkeeper with the caustic turn of phrase picked on the transitional, not to say tottering, state of affairs at Selhurst Park and observed, "The only way Palace will get into Europe will be if Dario writes 'em a song!"

I remember the emergence of an up-and-coming Birmingham comedian with

DINNER

strong affiliations to St. Andrews. Jasper Carrott with his now familiar guitar speculated with cynical humour on the development of more and more competitions in our already crowded calendar. He had the diners in stitches with his nightmare concept of the "Cup Winners' Cup Winners Cup!"

Yes, the comedy ingredient is vital. But the successful television production has hinged on far bigger headaches than choosing the right after-dinner entertainers. The problem is that a late night Sunday in London is not regarded as the best start to a week for their players by a lot of Managers, especially those from distant parts, and those still chasing major trophies. And it tends to be just those players that we need to ensure attend the dinner. There can be no greater anti-climax than building up to a main award and then having to announce that the winner is not present to receive it. But that really doesn't interest the Managers involved. And, over the years, what trouble we've had to set up the Player of the Year!

In 1977 Ron Saunders refused to allow Andy Gray to make the journey to London to receive the Young Player and the Player of the Year Awards — the only time one man has won both. So, an outside broadcast had to be mounted at Andy's home to link him up with the dinner and the waiting millions watching television. Two years ago, Bob Paisley would only allow the three Liverpool players nominated in the top six to be at the dinner if they flew down in a specially chartered plane, and winged their way home immediately afterwards. And this year, the rest of his Southampton team-mates had already departed for a Middle East 'break' when Kevin Keegan made his detour to London to collect the trophy. It involved a postponement of Southampton's first tour match and an early-morning dash to Heathrow for Kevin on the Monday morning!

And, as if that particular part of the proceedings didn't take enough arranging with Lawrie McMenemy, the Young Player of the Year was Steve Moran — and he was injured and unable to travel to the dinner! This was where it became like a 'This Is Your Life' programme. Lawrie played his part magnificently. The youngster was called in to join his team-mates for their usual pre-match lunch and the look on his face when Kevin Beattie walked in to present him with his award made all the pressures and finger-crossing worthwhile.

That moment when the name comes out of the envelope always has a little bit of magic to it. Last year, the winner **had** to come from the Ipswich party. Three of them were nominated and Fran Thyssen was favourite. But when John Wark pipped him, the Ipswich table rose as a man, and enjoyed **his** moment as much as if it had been their own.

Despite the best efforts of those branches of the media that choose to try and ruin that moment for television and the player involved, most presentations **are** a complete surprise. The reactions and heartfelt words, sometimes barely choked out, prove that. It must be the loneliest place in the world — that stage, at that moment. But then that's the price you pay for reaching the top. Like the gentleman said, "It's the supreme accolade..."

SUPER SPORTS USA

A roll on the drums, a fanfare on six golden trumpets, and into the arena marches a troupe of high-stepping teenagers who are adding the dazzle to the razzmatazz of American sport.

World of Sport has taken viewers to the ringside of U.S. prize fights, to the beaches below towering rocks to witness high diving spectaculars, and into the super stadiums to sample America's own favourites, grid-iron football, and baseball.

Like most of life in America, sport is well planned, superbly presented, and watched by millions, either live in massive indoor and outdoor stadia, or on television. In the United States there is actually an all-sport channel on T.V. which transmits nothing else but sporting programmes.

Armchair fans can be taken to the ringside, out onto the fairways, or into the super-bowls for a feast of sport second to none.

But there is a change on the horizon. Up to a few years ago American style football, basketball, and baseball were the most popular television sports, along with other U.S. favourites like ice-hockey, and golf, but now another sport is taking over on the T.V. screens, and it has its roots in Britain.

Indoor soccer — we call it five-a-side — is proving even more popular than the full scale game, and the American's love it! So watch out America — here come the British!

Mr Versatile times two. Above Nottingham Forest and England goalkeeper Peter Shilton shows his all-round skills in this remarkable picture study of his super saving style.

Peter went to Forest after following in the footsteps of Gordon Banks at Leicester City and Stoke City, and only fate has prevented him from having a similar career to the 1966 World Cup hero.

With rivals like Ray Clemence and Joe Corrigan around, Peter has had to fight for his international appearances, while he would have been an automatic choice at other times.

MR VERSATILE X 2

When it comes to fighting you can't beat a man like Daley Thompson

The decathlete really is as versatile in the athletics stadium as Peter is dependable in goal.

After taking the Olympic Gold in the ten-event competition with 8,495 points, Daley set a new World record in 1982 to reach 8,707 — 58 more than the previous best.

What really is remarkable about Daley's all round ability is that he could probably represent his country at any of the ten sections of the decathlon.

He turned to his speciality at 16, and now eight years later he is at the top of his trade.

While Peter Shilton might have had problems establishing himself as England's number one goalkeeper, Daley Thompson is first choice in the decathlon, and intends to stay that way.

"I would like to win another Olympic Gold in Los Angeles in 1984, and perhaps another in 1988 when the games are held in Seoul — even if that means training five or six hours a day for seven days a week," he says.

With both men dedicated to personal fitness and determined to achieve perfection in their sport any medals they pick up on the way are an added bonus.

KEVIN KEEGAN

2 WAYS OF LEAVING THE FIELD

...Jubilation

...Disgrace

ANSWERS

Did you reach the top in our sporting quiz? Check your answers below scoring a point for every rung you reached on the ladder.

Three rungs: Fair
Six rungs: Good
Nine rungs: Very good
Thirteen rungs: Clever aren't you!

Answers: 1, Peter Withe; 2, Dean, partner in the ice dance world championship duo; 3, World champion dart thrower Jocky Wilson; 4, 147; 5, Aberdeen beat Glasgow Rangers 4-1 (after extra-time); 6, Scotland World Cup Skipper Danny McGrain; 7, Brazil — it was presented to them after winning their third World championship. The World Cup now played for is the F.I.F.A. Cup; 8, Cricketer Glenn is a New Zealander. He was born in Dunedin; 9, Golfing superstar Jack Nicklaus; 10, American ace Kenny Roberts; 11, Liverpool's Bob Paisley; 12, 26 miles 385 yards; 13, 1982 Derby winners Pat Eddery, and Golden Fleece.

Answer to page 18

Yes, you were right, it is of course Lester Piggott.

Aintree Racecourse.